THE DEATH OF
KAREN SILKWOOD

The difference between a true story and a fictional one is this: a fictional story has an ending, but a true story does not. When we have read the last page of a fictional story, we know everything: there is nothing more to discover. In a true story, there is always more to find out, because we can never know it all.

Peop... It
can... es
muc...

Thi... d.
Her... ld,
old... n't
kno... the
rea... f it
wa... nd
we... ca,
an...

OXFORD BOOKWORMS LIBRARY

True Stories

The Death of Karen Silkwood

Stage 2 (700 headwords)

Series Editor: Jennifer Bassett
Founder Editor: Tricia Hedge
Activities Editors: Jennifer Bassett and Alison Baxter

JOYCE HANNAM

The Death of
Karen Silkwood

OXFORD UNIVERSITY PRESS

OXFORD
UNIVERSITY PRESS

Great Clarendon Street, Oxford OX2 6DP

Oxford University Press is a department of the University of Oxford.
It furthers the University's objective of excellence in research, scholarship,
and education by publishing worldwide in

Oxford New York

Auckland Cape Town Dar es Salaam Hong Kong Karachi
Kuala Lumpur Madrid Melbourne Mexico City Nairobi
New Delhi Shanghai Taipei Toronto

With offices in

Argentina Austria Brazil Chile Czech Republic France Greece
Guatemala Hungary Italy Japan Poland Portugal Singapore
South Korea Switzerland Thailand Turkey Ukraine Vietnam

OXFORD and OXFORD ENGLISH are registered trade marks of
Oxford University Press in the UK and in certain other countries

This edition © Oxford University Press 2008

The moral rights of the author have been asserted

Database right Oxford University Press (maker)

First published in Oxford Bookworms 1991

8 10 9

ISBN 978 0 19 479057 4

A complete recording of this Bookworms edition of
The Death of Karen Silkwood is available on audio CD ISBN 978 0 19 478980 6

Printed in China

Photographs courtesy of: Capital Cities/ABC, Inc.

Word count (main text): 5585 words

For more information on the Oxford Bookworms Library,
visit www.oup.com/bookworms

CONTENTS

1

The accident

It was dark. Nobody saw the accident. The small white car was found on its side by the bridge. A river ran underneath the road there, and the car was lying next to the bridge wall, below the road. Inside the car was a dead woman. Her name was Karen Silkwood and she was twenty-eight years old. It was November 13th, 1974.

How did the car come off the road? Why was it on the wrong side of the road? Why was it so far from the road? There was nothing wrong with the car. Karen Silkwood was a good driver. Everybody knew that.

How did the car come off the road?

The police thought that there was an easy answer to these questions. Karen was tired after a long day, so she fell asleep while she was driving. It could happen to anyone very easily. They took the car to a garage and they took Karen's body to a hospital.

But some people were not happy about the accident. First of all, her boyfriend, Drew Stephens. Also a newspaper journalist from the *New York Times* and a Union official from Washington. These three men were waiting for Karen on the night of the accident. She was bringing them some papers and some photographs in a big brown envelope. The papers were very important. The men were waiting for Karen in a hotel room a few miles from the accident. But she never arrived. When they heard about the accident, the men looked for the brown envelope at once. They looked for it inside the white car. They looked for it at the hospital and at the police station. The next morning they looked all around the wall and in the river, but they never found it. Nobody ever found that brown envelope.

2

The new job

The story of Karen and her brown envelope began in 1972 when she took a new job at a nuclear factory in Oklahoma. Before that, she worked as a secretary, but in 1972 she was really tired of a secretary's life. She looked in the newspaper and saw that there was a job at the nuclear factory. The pay was much better than a secretary's pay, and the work was more interesting. She went to see Mr Bailey, the manager of the factory, and she was surprised and happy when he gave her the job immediately. He asked Karen to start work the next day.

On her first day at the factory Karen learnt a lot. Mr Bailey told her that she had to wear a special white coat, some special shoes and a white hat.

'These clothes protect you from radioactive dust,' he said. 'There isn't really any danger, of course. Everything is safe here. We check everything all the time.'

'I see,' said Karen.

'You need an identity card to get into the factory every morning. Just give me a photograph of you and I'll give you a card. A pretty picture of a pretty girl.'

He smiled. Karen didn't like that smile.

'He thinks I'm stupid,' she thought. 'Why do men always think that pretty girls are stupid?'

He was still speaking.

'Now I'll call Mrs Phillips. She'll take you round the factory and show you your laboratory. The manager there will explain the job to you. Don't worry – it's very easy.'

He smiled his thin smile again.

The door opened and Mrs Phillips came in. She was about forty years old and a little fat. She looked afraid.

'You wanted me, Mr Bailey?'

'Yes, Susan. This is Karen Silkwood. She's going to work with you in your laboratory. Could you take her round the factory and tell her about the work?'

'Oh, I see. Of course, Mr Bailey. Please follow me, Miss Silkwood.'

When the office door closed, Mrs Phillips smiled at Karen, and said,

'That was lucky! Usually if he calls me, he wants to shout at me about something. Please call me Susan. Can I call you Karen?'

'Of course,' said Karen.

They walked down a long corridor with heavy doors on both sides. Susan opened one of the doors.

'This is our laboratory.'

Karen saw six or seven people in the room. They were all wearing white gloves and their hands were inside a big glass box. There were holes in the side of the box – just big enough for hands. Everyone looked at Karen.

'What's in the box?' Karen asked Susan.

Everyone laughed.

'Not chocolate,' said one worker.

'Or beer,' said another.

'Don't listen to them,' said Susan. 'It's fuel rods and uranium. We put uranium into the fuel rods. That's why you must always wear your gloves. And when you leave the laboratory, always remember to take off your gloves and check your hands in front of the scanner.'

There were holes in the side – just big enough for hands.

She showed Karen the scanner, which was near the door.

'If there's any radioactive dust on your hands, the scanner knows at once. An alarm rings all over the factory.'

'And when the alarm rings, the party begins,' said one man.

'Party?' Karen asked.

'You can take off all your clothes and have a swim . . . with lots of water.'

'He means they wash you in a shower,' said Susan. 'It doesn't happen very often.'

Karen went home happy at the end of the day. She didn't think that the work was difficult. And the money was good . . . very good.

3

Karen and Drew

At first Karen liked her new job. She was an ordinary, small-town girl who liked ordinary things: a comfortable home, a glass of beer, an evening with good friends. Soon she had some new friends from the factory.

She also liked Drew. He worked in another part of the factory, but everyone used the same coffee bar. She met him a few days after she started the job. In the coffee bar she and Susan were laughing together at a story in the newspaper. Then Karen suddenly heard a voice behind her.

'Here's a new face.'

She turned round quickly. A tall man was standing just behind her chair with a coffee in his hand.

'Be careful with that coffee, will you?' said Karen. 'You're going to drop some on me in a moment.'

'It's too good to be true. Nobody as beautiful as you ever works in this factory. What about having a pizza with me tonight after work?'

Karen wasn't sure what to say. He looked nice, but she didn't know anything about him.

Susan understood what Karen was thinking.

'Don't worry, dear. It's only Drew. He's big and he doesn't talk much, but he's not dangerous.'

Drew laughed.

'Thanks, Susan. I'll buy you a coffee every day this week for that.'

He turned to Karen.

'Can I buy you a pizza or not? What do you say?'

Karen smiled.

'I never miss a free meal.'

When Karen arrived at the restaurant that evening, Drew was already there. He stood up when she came in and gave her a big friendly smile. Karen thought of Mr Bailey's smile. How could two smiles be so different?

Karen found that it was very easy to talk to Drew. He listened to what she said and they laughed at the same things. It was like talking to her favourite brother. In the next few weeks they spent a lot of time together. Everyone at the factory saw how happy they were. Life was going well for Karen.

In the next few weeks Karen and Drew spent a lot of time together.

4

The shower

But in the summer of 1974 everything began to change. One evening Karen and Susan were leaving the laboratory. First Karen checked her hands in front of the scanner, and then a minute later Susan checked her hands. Suddenly there was a terrible noise. It was like a high scream. Everybody could hear it all over the factory. Susan didn't move. She just looked at her hands. Then the door of the laboratory flew open. Two men in white coats ran in and took Susan by the arms. Before Karen could do anything, they pulled Susan through the door. The terrible noise of the alarm was still going. Karen shouted:

'Where are you taking her?'

Nobody could hear. Nobody answered. Suddenly the noise stopped. Karen turned to the other workers.

'Where will she be?'

'In the shower room.'

Karen ran out of the laboratory and along the corridor to the shower room.

Inside the room Susan was screaming. Karen pushed open the door.

Susan had no clothes on, and the two men were showering her from head to foot – in her eyes, inside her ears, everywhere. The water hit her body like stones.

'Stop that!' shouted Karen. 'You're hurting her.'

'Not as much as radioactive dust can hurt her. One very small piece could kill her,' shouted back one of the men.

Ten minutes later they stopped the shower. Susan's face was as white as snow and she was shaking with cold. The men checked her body again with a hand scanner.

'OK. You're clean now. Put your clothes on. In five minutes we'll come back and take you to the medical centre for more tests.'

They left. Susan looked at Karen.

'They say I'm clean. Outside perhaps. But what about inside? How much radioactive dust is in my body? Am I "hot"?'

Her voice was quiet and tired. Suddenly she looked old. Slowly, she began to put her clothes on.

'"Hot"? What do you mean?' asked Karen.

'"Hot" means radioactive.'

'I see.'

Karen looked at her own hands. Were they clean? How carefully did the scanner check them? She worked next to Susan in the laboratory. Perhaps the dust was on her hands, too.

'I'm sure you're fine, Susan. The men said you were OK. And the doctors will know.'

'Nobody knows. Uranium is very new. Nobody really

knows what it can do to us.'

One of the men came back with a woman.

'Come along, dear. Time for your medical tests.'

Then they saw Karen near the door.

'What are you doing here? If you've finished work for today, you can go home.'

Karen did not listen to them.

'Are you OK, Susan? Do you want me to come with you?'

Susan shook her head.

'No, it's OK. You go home, Karen. I'll phone you later. Don't worry about me. And thank you.'

The man and the woman took Susan's arms and walked down the corridor, with Susan between them. She looked very small and very afraid.

They took Susan's arms and walked down the corridor, with Susan between them.

5

The new union official

After the shower Susan was a different person. She was quiet and didn't laugh very often. One evening, a few months after the shower, Karen met Susan in a bar for a drink after work.

'You know, Karen, we really must leave the factory. It's very dangerous. How many times do we hear the alarm now? More and more often. And every time we hear it, we know that someone is in danger.'

'How does it happen? I don't understand it,' said Karen.

'It's because the factory is working twenty-four hours a day. The safety people can't do their job well. They have to check everything carefully every day, but when can they do it? When we finish, there are the people who come in to work at night. The managers don't care about the danger. They only care about the money. And you know, Karen, I'm just the same. I also have to think only of money. I have three children and my husband is dead. I need the money from the factory. It's more than I can get from any other job in Oklahoma. Three children are expensive, very expensive . . .'

'Of course,' answered Karen. 'I understand. Drew and I have talked about this. He's thinking about leaving, too.'

'It's OK for a young man, strong like Drew. He can get many other jobs. You could leave too, Karen. Why don't you?'

'Because I've decided to change things here. I like the job and I like the people who work here. The money is good. We just need to improve safety – that's all. Surely that's not difficult? We have to talk to the managers and tell them it's important. Do you know Bob in Laboratory 16? Well, don't laugh, but he's asked me to be on the Union Committee, and I'm going to try it.'

'But, Karen . . . you can't. You're a woman. There are no women on the Committee. The men won't vote for you,' said Susan.

'Perhaps not,' replied Karen. 'But what about you? Will you vote for me? Do you know how many women work for this factory? Hundreds. And why won't the men vote for me? Perhaps I'm the first woman who has asked for their vote.'

Susan smiled. 'Well . . .'

But she couldn't find a good answer to Karen's question.

A week later, when the workers had to vote for the new Committee, most of the women voted for Karen. And a lot of the men voted for her, too. They saw that she really wanted to change things at the factory, and everyone agreed with her that safety was very important. So Karen was now an official on the factory's Union Committee.

Most of the women voted for Karen.

6

The meeting in Washington

A month or two later the alarm sounded again. This time Karen was in front of the scanner. She went quietly with the men in white coats. But after her shower she asked them a lot of questions about safety in the factory. They didn't answer any questions. They just got angry.

They knew she was on the Union Committee and they were afraid of her. All the managers knew that Karen was on the Committee because she always had a notebook in her hand. In her notebook she wrote down all the scanner alarms, every shower and every other danger in the factory. She asked a lot of people a lot of questions and always wrote the answers in her notebook. The notebook was getting full.

In September 1974 the Union Committee had a meeting. Everybody could see that safety at the factory was getting worse. The Committee decided to write to the Union leaders in Washington and ask for help. Two days later there was a phone call from Washington. The leaders wanted to see the Union Committee immediately in Washington.

For Karen this journey to Washington was a big

Karen asked a lot of people a lot of questions.

adventure. She wanted to see The White House and all the other famous places in the first city of the USA, but she had very little free time. She spent nearly all the time at a long meeting.

At first the leaders just listened to what Karen and the others said about the factory. Their faces got more and more unhappy. Karen explained what was happening.

'The managers take photographs of the fuel rods to check that they are safe. But I know that they are secretly changing the negatives of the photographs. And why are they doing that? Because the photographs show that the rods are *not* safe.'

Suddenly one of the leaders said to Karen,

'Do you understand what you're saying, Miss Silkwood? The lives of many people could be in danger if you're right. Uranium is very, very dangerous.'

'I'm just telling you what the people in the photographic laboratory have told me,' Karen said.

'If this is true, the government will close your factory. Do you understand what that means? A lot of people will lose their jobs. The story will be on the front page of every newspaper.'

Karen looked unhappy. 'Will it? We only want the managers to change a few things and to be more careful about safety.'

'I think it's already too late for that.'

Karen spent nearly all the time at a long meeting.

After the meeting one of the leaders stopped Karen outside in the corridor.

'Just come with me for a minute, please,' he said.

He took Karen into a small room and closed the door. He didn't want anybody to hear them.

'Karen, we need proof about these negatives. Without proof nobody will believe our story. Can you get some for us?'

'What proof do you need?'

'Someone will have to go into the photographic laboratory and steal some negatives. We need the negatives both *before* they change them *and after* they change them. Do you know where they keep the negatives?'

'Yes, I know,' said Karen quietly. 'But it will be very difficult. I don't work in the photographic laboratory. If one of the managers sees me there, how can I explain what I'm doing?'

'I don't know, but you'll have to think of something. We can't help you if you haven't any proof.'

They were both silent for a minute. Karen looked out of the window. It was a lovely evening. She thought of Mr Bailey's cold smile and Susan's screams in the shower.

'I'll do it,' she said.

'Good girl. It will be very dangerous. Nobody must know what you're doing. Not your friends on the Committee – nobody. I'll be the only person who knows.

I'll phone you once a week and you can tell me how you're getting on.'

'Nobody? Can't I tell my boyfriend Drew?' asked Karen.

'No. It could be dangerous for anybody who knows.'

'I see. OK. I'll do what I can,' said Karen slowly.

'Be very, very careful. You're a brave girl. I'd like to thank you for agreeing to do this.'

Karen stood up. Outside the window the sun was still shining, but she felt cold and lonely.

'Can I phone you if I need to speak to someone?'

'Of course. Any time, day or night. This is my card with my name and phone number.'

Karen took his card. She saw that his name was Pete. She looked at him once more and then she left the room.

7

The brown envelope

When she arrived back from Washington, Drew was waiting at the airport.

'Did you have a good time?'

'Not really. Things are worse at the factory than we thought. The Union leaders are going to send some doctors to the factory to talk to everyone about the dangers of uranium.'

'Poor Karen. You look very tired. Let's go home, have a beer and listen to some music. Forget the factory for one evening.'

Karen looked at Drew's kind, strong face. She wanted so much to tell him . . . but no, she mustn't tell anybody. She tried to smile.

'OK. What about a pizza at our favourite restaurant?' she said.

During the month of October 1974 Karen told nobody about her secret, but she felt very lonely. She began to work at nights because there were fewer people working in the factory then, and so it was easier to get into the photographic laboratory. Very slowly and carefully, she began stealing negatives. She put the negatives in a brown envelope and put the envelope in a secret hole in the wall

Very slowly and carefully, Karen began stealing negatives.

of her house. Nobody knew it was there. In the daytime, when she was not at work, it was difficult to sleep. She was afraid all the time. She often felt that people were watching her.

Soon some doctors came from Washington and spoke to the workers. After that everyone tried to help Karen. They were really afraid when they heard about the dangers of uranium. Soon Karen had to begin a new notebook. Everywhere she went in the factory, the notebook went with her.

The managers watched Karen and they watched her notebook. One day she left it on a table in the coffee bar for two minutes while she went to get some sugar. A manager tried to take it, but the other workers stopped him.

'What are you doing? That's Karen's book.'

The manager's face turned red and he put the book down. But the managers were now watching her all the time. It was more and more difficult to get into the photographic laboratory. But in the last week of October Karen told the Union leader in Washington that she had nearly all the proof necessary.

'That's wonderful,' said Pete's soft voice in Washington. 'When you're ready, I'll take you to meet an important man from the *New York Times*. We'll give the story to the newspapers, and they'll tell the world about it. Then the government and the factory managers will have to do something about the dangers of your work.'

'Give me just a little more time,' said Karen. And she put down the telephone.

'We'll give the story to the newspapers,' said Pete's soft voice in Washington.

8

A 'hot' home

At the beginning of November Karen was ready for the meeting with the *New York Times* journalist. The brown envelope was full.

Then Drew decided to leave his job at the factory. He told Karen that the work was too dangerous. He wanted Karen to leave, too.

'Not yet,' Karen said. She wanted to stay until the meeting with the *New York Times*. She knew she would have to leave the factory after that. But how could she explain to Drew?

Karen was now working during the daytime again, and on the evening of November 6th she passed the scanner on her way out of the laboratory. Suddenly the alarm sounded. She had to have another shower. After the shower she went home, very tired and unhappy.

After she arrived home, she went to the bathroom for a quick wash and then she went to the kitchen to make a sandwich for the next morning at the factory. Then she went to bed.

The next morning, November 7th, she got up and went to work. She was still tired, and she forgot to take her

On her way into the laboratory Karen passed the scanner.

sandwich out of the fridge. On the way into her laboratory
she passed the scanner. Immediately the alarm sounded.
Everyone stopped what they were doing. The alarm never
went off when people arrived – only when they left . . .
Everyone looked at Karen.

'Perhaps the scanner's wrong,' said Susan.

But the men in white arrived and began to pull Karen
out of the room.

'No, please . . . not again. All my body hurts from the
shower last night . . .'

But nobody listened. They showered her again. But
after the shower she didn't pass the usual scanner test.

There was still something radioactive in her body.

'What does it mean?' asked Karen.

Nobody answered. A doctor arrived and checked the test again. He shook his head.

'Where were you last night?' he asked.

'Here,' said Karen. 'I was working late.'

'Where did you go after work?'

'Home, of course. I was tired so I went to bed.'

'Are you sure?'

'Sure? Of course I'm sure.'

'Did you see anyone?'

'Only the other girl in my house, Paula. I just said good night to her. She was already in bed.'

'OK . . . Let's go,' said one of the men in white.

'Where?'

'What's your address?'

'26 Third Avenue West . . . Why?'

'Get in the car. Don't ask stupid questions. We don't answer questions from thieves.'

'Thieves? What have I stolen?'

'Get into the car.'

Someone pushed Karen into a big white car. It was full of more men in white. They were all wearing the special white clothes and hats to protect their faces and bodies, and they were all holding scanners. They drove to Karen's home and opened the door with Karen's key.

'Stay in the car,' one of the men in white shouted at Karen.

But Karen didn't listen to him. She followed them to the house and looked through the windows. The men went all round the house with the scanners and everywhere was radioactive – the kitchen, the bedroom, the bathroom. The kitchen was very 'hot', and when the men opened the fridge, the noise from the scanners was very loud. The men followed the noise to the sandwich.

'I suppose she made this last night,' said one of the men. 'Stupid girl. She's lucky that nobody has eaten it.'

They put the sandwich carefully into a bag. That was only the beginning. Soon all Karen's things were in bags – her clothes, her books, her photos. When they took her

Soon all Karen's things were in bags.

photo of Drew, Karen couldn't stay quiet any longer.

'What are you doing? It's just a photo!'

'Be quiet!' they told her. 'Don't you understand anything? Your house is very radioactive. The walls are "hot" too. We can't leave anything in the house; it's not safe. Think of the people next door. Now we're going to lock the house and nobody must go in again. Phone your friend Paula and tell her to find somewhere to sleep tonight. Don't tell her too much. Nobody must know what's happened here. People won't understand and they'll begin to worry and get afraid. That's not good for the factory.'

'The factory . . . ? Who cares about the factory? What about me? If my house is radioactive, I'm radioactive too,' said Karen.

'Why didn't you think of that before you stole the uranium? Go to your boyfriend's house. Don't go out. Don't speak to anyone. We'll phone you tomorrow and tell you what to do.'

They put all the bags in the car and drove away. Karen stood alone in the middle of the street. They thought she was a thief. But why? Who could want to take uranium out of the factory? Everyone knew how stupid and dangerous that was. She looked silently at her empty house. Now there was nothing in her home – only a brown envelope in a hole in the wall.

9

Where to go?

Karen tried to think. She was 'hot'. Perhaps she was dying. She was dangerous to other people, dangerous to Drew. She couldn't phone him. She was alone. She forgot about Pete in Washington. She sat down on the ground and cried. She wanted to die quickly.

Three hours later Drew found her there. She was still sitting on the ground. Her face was white and empty. She didn't look up when he walked across to her.

'Karen, my Karen, come with me at once. Someone from the factory phoned me. I know everything. Karen . . . look at me.'

'Don't come near me. I'm dangerous to you.'

'Don't be stupid. I talked to the doctor at the factory. He says you're not dangerous to anyone. You've had a shower, so your body's not radioactive now.'

Karen looked up into his face. 'And you believe him? Do you still believe anybody in that place? Do you also believe I stole uranium from the factory?'

'Of course not. Did they say that to you? That's terrible! Wait until tomorrow. When I get in there, they'll be sorry they ever said that to you.'

Karen stood alone outside her empty house.

'It's no good, Drew, I'm dying,' said Karen quietly. 'I don't know how this happened, but I know one thing. There are people at that factory who want to see me dead.'

'Karen . . . you're tired. You need a holiday. You must leave the factory like me. Come home with me now.'

'Home? I haven't got a home any more.' Karen put her head in her hands.

Drew looked at the empty house. His face was white and angry.

'Did they do that, too? Karen . . . my home is your home from now on.'

He took both Karen's hands and pulled her to her feet. He helped her to his car, and took her home.

10

Karen explains to Drew

That night Karen and Drew couldn't sleep. They had to talk.

'How did your house get so radioactive? That's the question,' said Drew.

'I think,' answered Karen, 'that someone put something radioactive into my bag last night before I left the factory. I remember that I left my bag on the table for a few minutes at coffee time in the afternoon.'

'But, Karen, who did that? And why?'

'Drew, I'm going to tell you something. Perhaps I'm dying now, so there mustn't be any secrets between us any more. I agreed to get photos of the fuel rods for the Union in Washington. I've stolen photos and negatives from the photographic laboratory. Perhaps someone saw me . . . one of the managers.'

'You've stolen photos? What photos? Why?'

Karen explained everything to Drew. He was very quiet when she finished. In the end, he took her hand.

'Karen, this is very dangerous. I'm afraid for you. Perhaps someone does want to kill you. Didn't you think of that danger when the Union asked you to do this? Why did you agree to do it?'

That night Karen and Drew couldn't sleep. They had to talk.

'Because I care, Drew. Somebody has to do something. Why not me? I care about you, about Susan, about everyone who has ever worked at that factory. If the danger from radioactive dust doesn't stop, perhaps we'll all die. Don't you understand that?'

'Yes, I understand,' said Drew quietly. 'But I also understand that you're doing a difficult and dangerous job alone. You mustn't work alone any more. I'll be with you all the time. Nobody is going to hurt you again.'

Karen smiled.

'I was right to tell you. I need a friend, and you are the best friend that I have. But it's not much longer now. After the meeting with the *New York Times*, everything will be finished. I can go on for a few more days. But I'll tell you everything from now on.'

Next morning Karen telephoned Pete in Washington and the Union Committee at the factory. She told them about her house and that the managers were calling her a thief.

From Washington Pete's voice sounded angry and worried.

'The factory's managers are trying to sack you. Say nothing, do nothing. We'll speak to them and tell them that we know what's happened to you. You must have medical tests, and we'll tell them that.'

Karen waited at Drew's house all day. In the evening the phone rang.

Next morning Karen telephoned Pete in Washington.

'Miss Silkwood?' said Mr Bailey's cold voice. 'You and Drew and your friend Paula must go to Los Alamos for tests. The doctors there know all about uranium and radioactive dust. We've talked to the Union. We will pay for the journey and they will pay for the tests. But we know that you've stolen some uranium – that's why you were so radioactive. There's no other answer.'

The phone line went dead.

Karen looked at Drew.

'You and I are going to Los Alamos for medical tests. But I'm sure now . . . the managers know. They know what I've really stolen. And they'll look for them while we're away. They'll tell everyone that they're looking for the stolen uranium. But they won't find anything. They won't find their negatives.'

11

The night drive

Karen, Paula and Drew went to Los Alamos and had the tests. The doctors said that Karen's body was still a little radioactive, but Drew and Paula were all right. It was very good news. They told Karen that she was in no danger now. But they also explained that they didn't know about the future.

'It will be a few years,' they said, 'before we know that you're really all right.'

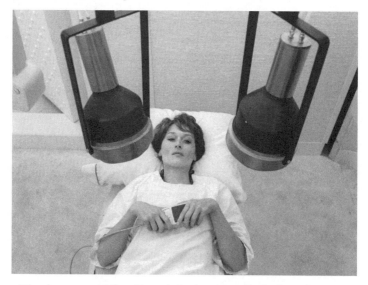

The doctors said that Karen's body was still a little radioactive.

High in the mountains around Los Alamos, Paula, Drew and Karen had a party in a little restaurant. Karen felt years younger. She was not going to die. She and Drew still had a future together. They all danced until midnight.

The next day they took the plane back to Oklahoma City. Karen had to go back because that evening there was a Union meeting at the factory and after that, her meeting with Pete and the journalist from the *New York Times*. It was an important day for her. They arrived at the airport in the morning. Early in the evening Karen drove to her house. She went alone because Drew was working. She used her key and went quietly into the house. She was only inside the house for three minutes and then she left immediately and went to the Union meeting at the factory.

That night at the meeting, Karen had a big brown envelope in her bag. The envelope was too big for the bag, so everyone could see it. All the workers were very happy to hear that Karen was all right. They were afraid that she was very ill, so when they saw her looking happy and well, everyone felt better.

'She looks as happy as she did a year ago,' thought Susan. 'A pretty, happy girl, who likes a good time and a good laugh.'

After the meeting a lot of people wanted to talk to Karen and ask her about the last few days.

'I'm sorry,' she said. 'I can't talk to you now.

I have to go to another meeting.'

'With your good-looking Drew?' asked someone with a friendly laugh.

'Yes,' said Karen. 'With Drew. And one or two other people.' She smiled.

'Can I take you in my car?' asked her friend Bob.

'No, thanks,' said Karen. 'I've got my car here.'

It was dark when Karen left the factory. She smiled at all her friends, got into her small white car and drove away.

Nobody ever found the brown envelope.

Karen never arrived at her meeting with Drew, Pete and the journalist from the *New York Times*. On the road to the meeting, a few miles from the nuclear factory, she had an accident by a wall near a river. It was November 13th, 1974. Nobody ever found the brown envelope.

GLOSSARY

alarm   a loud sound (often a bell) which tells people that there is danger

bar   a room where people can buy and have drinks

beer   an alcoholic drink

believe   to think that something is true

brave *(adj)*   not showing that you are afraid

care *(v)*   to feel interest in something or someone

check *(v)*   to look at something carefully to see if it is right, good, safe, etc.

committee   a group of people chosen by others to plan and organize for them

corridor   a long narrow passage with doors into rooms

envelope   a paper cover for a letter or other papers

fridge (refrigerator)   a kind of cupboard which keeps food cold

fuel rods   metal tubes which contain uranium

gloves   covers for the hands

government   the group of people who control a country

identity card   a card with your photograph on it, which shows who you are

journalist   a person who writes for newspapers

laboratory   a building or room where scientists work

leader   someone who is the most important person in a group, a government, a union, etc.

manager   someone who controls a business, a factory, a bank, etc.

medical   connected with medicine, doctors, hospital, etc.

negatives   pieces of film from which we make photographs

nuclear a kind of energy made by breaking the central part of an atom into two pieces

official *(n)* someone who does important work for a union, a government, etc.

ordinary not strange or special

pretty nice-looking, lovely

proof anything which shows, or helps to show, that something is true

protect to keep someone or something safe

radioactive dust very, very small pieces of broken atoms which come from nuclear materials or explosions

sack *(v)* to make someone leave his/her job

safe *(adj)* not in danger

safety being safe

scanner a machine which can see very small things on or inside the body, which the human eye cannot see

shower a place where you can wash under water that falls from above

suppose to think that something is true when you are not sure

test *(n)* looking at something carefully to find out more about it

union a group of workers who join together to talk to managers about their pay, hours of work, etc.

uranium [U] a heavy grey metal that sends out radioactive waves, and is used to make nuclear energy

vote *(v)* to choose someone in an election by marking a piece of paper

worried *(adj)* afraid that something is, or will be, bad or wrong

worry *(v)* to feel afraid and that something is, or will be, bad or wrong

The Death of Karen Silkwood

ACTIVITIES

Before Reading

1 Read the story introduction on the first page of the book, and the back cover. How much do you know now about *The Death of Karen Silkwood*? Tick one box for each sentence.

	YES	NO	PERHAPS
1 Karen wanted to say something important.	☐	☐	☐
2 Some people were afraid of Karen.	☐	☐	☐
3 This is a true story.	☐	☐	☐
4 The story happened in England.	☐	☐	☐
5 Karen worked in Oklahoma.	☐	☐	☐
6 Karen's death was an accident.	☐	☐	☐
7 We know what happened to Karen.	☐	☐	☐

2 What is going to happen in the story? Can you guess? Tick one box for each sentence.

	YES	NO
1 Karen works as a police officer.	☐	☐
2 Karen wants to help people.	☐	☐
3 Karen steals something.	☐	☐
4 Karen kills somebody.	☐	☐
5 Karen dies in her car.	☐	☐

While Reading

Read Chapters 1 and 2. Write answers to these questions.

1 How old was Karen when she died?
2 Why were some men waiting for her on the night that she died?
3 In her new job at the nuclear factory, what did Karen have to wear?
4 What happened when there was radioactive dust on someone's hands?

Read Chapters 3 and 4. Are these sentences true (T) or false (F)? Rewrite the false ones with the correct information.

1 Karen met Drew in the coffee bar at the factory.
2 Karen and Drew were unhappy together.
3 When Karen checked her hands in front of the scanner, the alarm made a noise.
4 Susan had to have a shower.
5 After her shower, Susan went home.

Read Chapters 5 and 6, then answer these questions.

Who

1 . . . wanted to stop working in the factory?
2 . . . decided to change things in the factory?
3 . . . voted for Karen to be on the Union Committee?
4 . . . always carried a notebook?
5 . . . wrote to the Union leaders in Washington?
6 . . . took photographs of the fuel rods?
7 . . . asked Karen to steal some photograph negatives?

Read Chapters 7 and 8. Who said this, and to whom?

1 'Things are worse at the factory than we thought.'
2 'That's Karen's book.'
3 'We'll give the story to the newspapers and they'll tell the world about it.'
4 'Perhaps the scanner's wrong.'
5 'Where were you last night?'
6 'Get into the car.'

Before you read Chapters 9 and 10, can you guess the answers to these questions?

1 Why is Karen's house radioactive?
2 Will Karen tell Drew the truth?
3 Will Pete help Karen?
4 What will Mr Bailey tell Karen to do?

Read Chapters 9 and 10. Put these sentences in the correct order.

1 The next morning Karen telephoned Pete.

2 Karen told Drew about the photographs.

3 Mr Bailey told Karen that she must go for medical tests.

4 Drew came to find Karen.

5 Karen waited at Drew's house all day.

6 Drew took Karen back to his house.

Read Chapter 11. Choose the best question-word for these questions and then answer them.

How / What / Where

1 . . . did the doctors say about Karen?

2 . . . did Karen feel then?

3 . . . was the Union meeting?

4 . . . did Karen have in her bag at the meeting?

5 . . . did Karen go after the meeting?

6 . . . did Karen die?

Which answer to this question do you prefer?

What happened to the brown envelope?

1 It fell in the river after the accident.

2 It fell out of Karen's bag when she left the factory.

3 Someone stole it from Karen's car after the accident.

4 You choose!

After Reading

1 **The police came to tell Drew about Karen's accident. Write out the conversation in the correct order and put in the speakers' names. The policeman speaks first (number 8).**

1 _____ 'What kind of an accident? Where is she?'

2 _____ 'But she was a good driver. Was something wrong with the car?'

3 _____ 'We found her car lying on its side below the road, next to the bridge wall.'

4 _____ 'What's happened to her?'

5 _____ 'We didn't find any papers, sir.'

6 _____ 'No, nothing. She was tired. She probably fell asleep while she was driving. It happens very easily.'

7 _____ 'You mean that she's dead? What happened?'

8 _____ 'I'm afraid we have some bad news about your girlfriend, sir.'

9 _____ 'She's had an accident, in her car.'

10 _____ 'I'm going to look for them myself.'

11 _____ 'But she was coming to meet me. She had some important papers with her.'

12 _____ 'We took her to the hospital. But I'm afraid it was too late.'

2 Here is a possible ending to the story. Match these parts of sentences and put them in the correct order to make a paragraph of eight sentences. Use these linking words. (You will need to use some of them more than once.)

and / and then / so / when

1 . . . opened the door of Karen's car.

2 A man got out of the other car

3 . . . died.

4 . . . she drove faster.

5 He took the brown envelope from Karen's bag,

6 Her car left the road

7 It was dark

8 . . . began to hit the back of her car again and again.

9 Karen hit her head

10 . . . she saw the lights of another car behind her.

11 Karen was very frightened

12 . . . turned over on its side.

13 She was driving carefully along the road to the hotel

14 . . . he drove away.

15 The car came right up behind Karen

16 . . . Karen left the factory.

3 Which story ending do you prefer? The one in Activity 1, or the one in Activity 2? Explain why.

4 There are 11 words from the story hidden in this word
search. Can you find them all? Words can only run from top
to bottom and from left to right.

X	S	Y	B	C	A	G	L	F	E	T
B	C	A	S	G	L	O	V	E	S	N
R	A	D	I	O	A	C	T	I	V	E
I	N	G	U	S	R	N	R	Q	U	G
V	N	N	W	F	M	Z	P	H	N	A
S	E	U	R	A	N	I	U	M	E	T
K	R	C	I	B	J	D	M	S	O	I
C	W	L	S	H	O	W	E	R	T	V
F	U	E	L	R	O	D	C	V	U	E
G	L	A	B	O	R	A	T	O	R	Y
M	T	R	A	V	A	P	H	O	T	O

5 Do you agree (A) or disagree (D) with these sentences?
Explain why.

1 Karen was right to become a Union official.
2 Pete was wrong to ask Karen to steal the negatives.
3 Karen was stupid to steal the negatives.
4 Drew didn't protect Karen enough.
5 The managers cared more about making money than
about safety.
6 The Union didn't protect Karen enough.

6 Use the chart to write sentences about these people. Join your sentences with *and* where possible.

		big and strong
		a thin smile
		pretty
Karen		a little fat
Drew	is	a friendly smile
Susan	has	three children
Mr Bailey		twenty-eight years old
		brave
		about forty years old
		a cold voice

7 What do you know about nuclear energy? Find the answers to these questions.

1 Are there nuclear factories in your country?
2 Do you think that nuclear factories are a good way to make energy?
3 Do you know of any other ways to make energy?
4 Do you think that nuclear factories are usually safe?
5 Do you know about any accidents at nuclear factories?

ABOUT THE AUTHOR

Joyce Hannam is an experienced teacher and lecturer. She has taught English in several European countries, including Greece, Spain, Turkey, and the Czech Republic. She now lives in York, in the north of England, and works mostly with Japanese university students and business people from Germany, Italy, France, and Spain. Her stories for the Oxford Bookworms Library also include *Christmas in Prague* (at Stage 1).

For her story about Karen Silkwood she used information from books and from the well-known film. Karen Silkwood was a real person, who was born in 1946 and died in 1974, aged 28 years. There is still a mystery about her death in a car accident, and perhaps we will never know the real story of her death.

Joyce Hannam is married to a musician and has one young daughter. All three of them enjoy singing at all times and in all places.

OXFORD BOOKWORMS LIBRARY

Classics • Crime & Mystery • Factfiles • Fantasy & Horror
Human Interest • Playscripts • Thriller & Adventure
True Stories • World Stories

The OXFORD BOOKWORMS LIBRARY provides enjoyable reading in English, with a wide range of classic and modern fiction, non-fiction, and plays. It includes original and adapted texts in seven carefully graded language stages, which take learners from beginner to advanced level. An overview is given on the next pages.

All Stage 1 titles are available as audio recordings, as well as over eighty other titles from Starter to Stage 6. All Starters and many titles at Stages 1 to 4 are specially recommended for younger learners. Every Bookworm is illustrated, and Starters and Factfiles have full-colour illustrations.

The OXFORD BOOKWORMS LIBRARY also offers extensive support. Each book contains an introduction to the story, notes about the author, a glossary, and activities. Additional resources include tests and worksheets, and answers for these and for the activities in the books. There is advice on running a class library, using audio recordings, and the many ways of using Oxford Bookworms in reading programmes. Resource materials are available on the website <www.oup.com/bookworms>.

The *Oxford Bookworms Collection* is a series for advanced learners. It consists of volumes of short stories by well-known authors, both classic and modern. Texts are not abridged or adapted in any way, but carefully selected to be accessible to the advanced student.

You can find details and a full list of titles in the *Oxford Bookworms Library Catalogue* and *Oxford English Language Teaching Catalogues*, and on the website <www.oup.com/bookworms>.

THE OXFORD BOOKWORMS LIBRARY
GRADING AND SAMPLE EXTRACTS

STARTER • 250 HEADWORDS

present simple – present continuous – imperative –
can/cannot, must – going to (future) – simple gerunds …

Her phone is ringing – but where is it?

Sally gets out of bed and looks in her bag. No phone. She looks under the bed. No phone. Then she looks behind the door. There is her phone. Sally picks up her phone and answers it. *Sally's Phone*

STAGE 1 • 400 HEADWORDS

… past simple – coordination with *and, but, or* –
subordination with *before, after, when, because, so* …

I knew him in Persia. He was a famous builder and I worked with him there. For a time I was his friend, but not for long. When he came to Paris, I came after him – I wanted to watch him. He was a very clever, very dangerous man. *The Phantom of the Opera*

STAGE 2 • 700 HEADWORDS

… present perfect – *will* (future) – *(don't) have to, must not, could* –
comparison of adjectives – simple *if* clauses – past continuous –
tag questions – *ask/tell* + infinitive …

While I was writing these words in my diary, I decided what to do. I must try to escape. I shall try to get down the wall outside. The window is high above the ground, but I have to try. I shall take some of the gold with me – if I escape, perhaps it will be helpful later. *Dracula*

STAGE 3 • 1000 HEADWORDS

... should, may – present perfect continuous – *used to* – past perfect –
causative – relative clauses – indirect statements ...

Of course, it was most important that no one should see
Colin, Mary, or Dickon entering the secret garden. So Colin
gave orders to the gardeners that they must all keep away
from that part of the garden in future. *The Secret Garden*

STAGE 4 • 1400 HEADWORDS

... past perfect continuous – passive (simple forms) –
would conditional clauses – indirect questions –
relatives with *where/when* – gerunds after prepositions/phrases ...

I was glad. Now Hyde could not show his face to the world
again. If he did, every honest man in London would be proud
to report him to the police. *Dr Jekyll and Mr Hyde*

STAGE 5 • 1800 HEADWORDS

... future continuous – future perfect –
passive (modals, continuous forms) –
would have conditional clauses – modals + perfect infinitive ...

If he had spoken Estella's name, I would have hit him. I was so
angry with him, and so depressed about my future, that I could
not eat the breakfast. Instead I went straight to the old house.
Great Expectations

STAGE 6 • 2500 HEADWORDS

... passive (infinitives, gerunds) – advanced modal meanings –
clauses of concession, condition

When I stepped up to the piano, I was confident. It was as if I
knew that the prodigy side of me really did exist. And when I
started to play, I was so caught up in how lovely I looked that
I didn't worry how I would sound. *The Joy Luck Club*

Agatha Christie, Woman of Mystery

JOHN ESCOTT

What does the name 'Agatha Christie' mean? To many people, it means a book about a murder mystery – a 'whodunnit'. 'I'm reading an Agatha Christie,' people say. 'I'm not sure who the murderer is – I think it's ...' But they are usually wrong, because it is not easy to guess the murderer's name before the end of the book.

But who was Agatha Christie? What was she like? Was her life quiet and unexciting, or was it full of interest and adventure? Was there a mystery in her life, too?

Death in the Freezer

TIM VICARY

Ellen Shore's family is an ordinary American family, and Ellen is six years old when her brother Al is born. Her parents are very pleased to have a son, but Ellen is not pleased, because now baby Al comes first.

And when they are adults, Al still comes first. He begins a rock band and makes records. Soon he is rich and famous – very rich, but he gives nothing to his sister Ellen. She has a difficult life, with three young kids and very little money. And she learns to hate her rich, famous, unkind brother ...